CESAR CHAVEZ
CHANGING LIVES

WRITTEN BY PATRICE GOTSCH
ILLUSTRATED BY GIL ARREOLA

To all the people who have dedicated their
lives to making the world a better place.

Patrice Gotsch

To my right hand man, my father, a successful
immigrant who showed me the way.

Gil Arreola

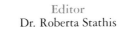

Editor
Dr. Roberta Stathis

Art Direction and Design
Danielle Arreola

Editorial Staff
Kristin Belsher
Linda Mammano
Rebecca Ratnam
Nina Chun

Printing Coordinator
Cathy Sanchez

Ballard & Tighe

Copyright ©2005 Ballard & Tighe, Publishers, a division of Educational IDEAS, Inc.

All rights reserved. No part of this publication may be reproduced in whole or in part, or stored in a retrieval system, or transmitted in any form or by any means, electronic or mechanical, including photocopy, recording, or otherwise, without permission in writing from the publisher.

Catalog # 2-375 • ISBN 1-55501-780-0 • 2005 Printing

Juana Chavez taught her children to help people who were less fortunate. She also taught them not to use violence against others. These two lessons guided Cesar Chavez throughout his life.

Humble Beginnings

Cesar Chavez was born March 31, 1927 near Yuma, Arizona. He was born in an apartment above his parents' grocery store. When Cesar was 10 years old, the country was experiencing very difficult financial problems.

Moving to California

Throughout the United States, many people lost their jobs. Cesar's family had to sell their farm in order to pay their taxes. Shortly after this happened, the Chavez family moved to California.

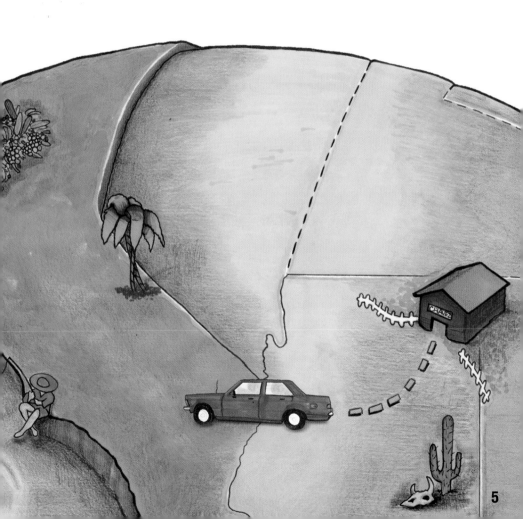

Working in the Fields

In California, the Chavez family worked on many different farms. They planted and picked crops on these farms. People who do this kind of work are called **migrant workers**. The farm owners did not want to pay migrant workers very much money. The Chavez family and other migrant workers needed jobs. As a result, they were willing to work for very little money.

migrant worker: a farm
worker who moves from
place to place to pick crops

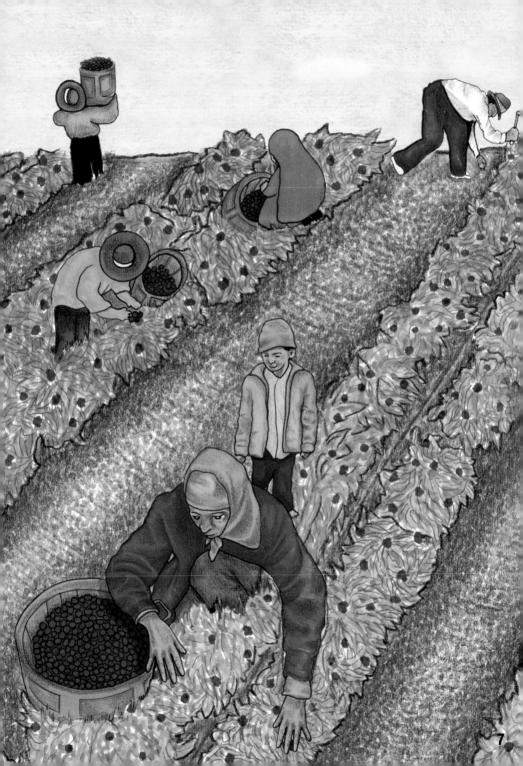

Picking Crops Under the Hot Sun

Every day the Chavez family picked crops such as grapes, cucumbers, and peaches under the hot California sun. They received only a small amount of money each week.

On the Move

The Chavez family did not have a permanent home in California. Sometimes they slept in their car. Cesar's family moved around so much that he was always changing schools. He had attended more than 30 different schools by the time he was in eighth grade.

Facing Prejudice

Many teachers and students were **prejudiced** against Mexican-American people and did not treat Cesar well. Cesar left school after eighth grade.

prejudiced: having an opinion, usually unfavorable, formed before the facts are known

Seeing Racism

Cesar joined the U.S. Navy when he was a teenager. Cesar saw **racism** everywhere—at school, in the Navy, in movie theaters, and in restaurants. He saw signs that said, "No dogs or Mexicans allowed."

racism: feelings or actions of hatred toward a person or persons because of their race

The Power to Make Changes

Chavez married a woman named Helen Fabela in 1948. The two of them moved around California looking for jobs. Around this time, Chavez's life began to change. He realized that he had the power to change his life and the lives of other migrant workers.

Empowering Migrant Workers

First, Chavez helped migrant workers become citizens. Then he helped them register to vote. He knew these actions would **empower** them. They could vote for people who cared about their problems and would help fix these problems.

empower: to give
power or authority to

Forming a Farm Workers Union

In 1962, Chavez decided to form a **union** for migrant workers. He thought an organized group could improve working conditions for migrant workers. Chavez's plans were not easy on his family. Helen had to work in the fields to make money for the family.

union: an organization of workers

Organizing the Union

Chavez met with individual workers and told them of his plans. Then he met with small groups of workers. In time, he held large meetings. Chavez named his union the National Farm Workers Association (NFWA). By 1965, 1,200 migrant families were part of this union.

The Grape Strike

The union held a big meeting and the workers who picked grapes decided to **strike**. Chavez believed that change could come through nonviolent actions. He sent workers all over the country. Their message was simple. They told people, "Don't buy grapes!" Workers also went on a march that was more than 300 miles to the California state capital. This march brought more attention to their cause.

strike: to stop working as a group to get better pay and working conditions

Victory at Last!

The grape strike lasted for five years. Finally, some owners agreed to pay the farm workers more money and improve their working conditions. Soon other workers joined Cesar Chavez. They established a union called the United Farm Workers of America (UFW). More owners agreed to meet the union's demands. When the strike was over, union workers were picking about 85% of California's grapes. This was a victory for Cesar Chavez and his union.

Nonviolent Methods

Cesar Chavez spent the rest of his life using nonviolent methods to improve the lives of farm workers. Once he **fasted** for 36 days to show his support for the workers.

fast: to stop eating for a period of time

A Life Dedicated to Change

Throughout his life, Chavez remembered two very important lessons that his mother taught him. He dedicated his life to helping others. And he created change through nonviolent actions. He was an inspiration to many other people who wanted to change the world around them. Cesar Chavez died on April 23, 1993, but people continue to be inspired by his ideas and actions.